If You Could Hear My Heart

Liberty Ramsay

BookLeaf Publishing

India | USA | UK

Presentation by *BookLeaf Publishing*

Web: www.bookleafpub.com

E-mail: info@bookleafpub.com

ISBN: 9789358314533

First edition 2023

Rough Edges

My heart has been torn
You kept the smooth side
Sliding it out of me, no harm to you
Now I'm left with my part
Uneven, deflated, incomplete,
With rough edges

Full...

I feel full….
When you message,
Replying after too long of me waiting
When our clothes brush against each other
When I feel that your blue eyes are staring into
my soul
When your around
You make my heart full

Diluted

The whole of my inner being,
Under my skin, through my veins, on my mind
24/7
Is so full of you,
I am being diluted

Strumming my heart

Every time we make eye contact
It is as if you're reaching your hands into my
chest
Strumming my heart like a ukulele
With your strong fingers

Stunned

My heart feels stunned.
Beating fast, uncontrollably
Unsettled in its empty cave
Echoing the noise of lonely fear

Moths

You make me nervous
I feel the butterflies,
Though it feels sort of different
Slightly worse than usual
Maybe its more like moths,
Eating me from the inside out

War

As I listen to the rain
My music in the background
It reminds me of the small joys,
No distractions
Peace
Until you reappear in my brain,
so vivid, stronger than ever
Just as I thought the war was over

Dreamer

Oh how could I ever be obsessed
with someone new
when every night
I dream of you

You, and only you
In a world where I could kiss you
Hug you, hold you in my arms
so I hope to never wake up
for the sake of living in my dreams

Falling

I fell for you
I fell so hard for you
That every part of my body
Will be forever bruised
Aching, throbbing

The Best

you're the best thing
the best thing that's ever happened to me
therefore I would not swap you out for anyone
and would go through the pain again and again
just to know you

The Fire

As I stand by the fire
surrounded by many people
a sense of peace and internal warmth
a Saturday night to feel myself,
no work tomorrow
a period of time to ponder on my thoughts
and contemplate all the future decisions to be
made
currently out of my control

Summer

as I step out into the fresh morning air there is a
distinct smell
the sweet scents of freshly mown grass
and the sense of neighbors pools being set up
long awaited,
ready for a good run,
ready for summer

Fresh Air

I love the fresh air
clearing the head
to focus on nature,
all the little things
that we're meant to notice
like the beautiful flowers that could make a day

a Home

Home,
you can live in a house
its not necessarily your home.
Home is the warm and fuzzy feeling on a cold
day,
the smell of sweet spices and cooking
lingering in the walls of a loving
Home

A typical Winter

Winter,
a good old winter morning
the thought of knowing you don't have to do
anything in a rush
managing a small sleep in,
watching a movie with a cozy rug in front of the
fireplace
giving the best warm and fuzzy feeling
you could get on a winter morning
its a typical winter morning

The flowers

growing everywhere
so many lovely flowers
how often do we notice them?
not enough

A good start

A good bakery
the most delicious smell your could come across
the sweet aroma of brioche cooking
slowly lingering in the air
a nice morning start

Blooms

I love spring
aside from hay fever
it brings out the love of nature
nothings dying
nothings drowning or burning
it's in its prime
Blooming